upside down and all around

gigi miller

This book is a work of fiction. The names, characters and events in this book are the products of the author's imagination or are used fictitiously. Any similarity to real persons living or dead is coincidental and not intended by the author.

The views and opinions expressed in this book are solely those of the author and do not reflect the views or opinions of Gatekeeper Press. Gatekeeper Press is not to be held responsible for and expressly disclaims responsibility for the content herein.

Upside Down and All Around

Published by Gatekeeper Press
7853 Gunn Hwy., Suite 209
Tampa, FL 33626
www.GatekeeperPress.com

Copyright © 2023 by Gigi Miller
All rights reserved. Neither this book, nor any parts within it may be sold or reproduced in any form or by any electronic or mechanical means, including information storage and retrieval systems, without permission in writing from the author. The only exception is by a reviewer, who may quote short excerpts in a review.

The typesetting and editorial work for this book are entirely the product of the author. Gatekeeper Press did not participate in and is not responsible for any aspect of these elements.

Cover Photography Robert Sturman
Set in Helvetica Neu and Baskerville

Library of Congress Control Number: 2024932413

ISBN (hardcover): 9781662945298
ISBN (paperback): 9781662945304
eISBN: 9781662945311

contents

part one
ALOHA SUN

I See *5*

The Trapeze *6*

Climb *7*

Do You Didgeridoo *8*

Here *9*

Grateful For *10*

Mana *11*

I can hear Ocean *12*

Grateful *13*

part two
MAHALO SUN

There Are *15*

A Diddy For Us *16*

Swimming *17*

The Ocean *18*

Whistle A Whistle *20*

A Day *21*

Grateful *22*

It's A Moment *23*

I Love You Like The Rain *24*

Time *25*

I Love to Write *26*

Moment *27*

Home *28*

Afar *29*

A Promise to Promise *30*

part three
ALOHA SUN

Sunset *32*

Chi *33*

It's A Light *34*

She Does *35*

Let's Phone *36*

And When Your Night Starts Making Sense *37*

A Lighthouse Keeper *38*

Maui Maui *39*

Re Viewing *40*

If I Had One Wish *42*

This Night *43*

aloha sun

part one

I See

I see a passageway
Through the calm rapids.
I see a way through
It's different every day.

The Trapeze

Fills the breeze of ease.
I feel a gentle smile
Climb up my face.
It's whirling and surfing
Through waves
That crash and tumult.
It's the rhythm of a heart
That stops
In a moment of passion.
When I see smiles
I smile too.
Inside I am grateful
For the negativity
To transform
From pity
To gratitude.

Climb

To the top of a mountain.
Frolic to the edge of the sea!
Welcome the day with love
And respect.
A meadow of light
That nourishes.
Let go of the past
It clouds the beauty
Of this moment.
If the past
Appears…
Welcome it and
Breathe.
It passes from the past
To a place of loveliness
That resides
In the moment.

Do You Didgeridoo

Can you sing a tune too?
Do you fiddle on the fiddle?
And rhyme just a little
Do you skip in the day?
To then spin, sit and giggle
Do you simply say…
Thank you?
I like to wiggle and giggle
With a tribe
That giggles kindly.
The kind that listens
To the sunshine.

Here

Where fun is to be had.
It's a time in the moment
Spontaneous.
A joke or a whisper,
A gentle nod.
A plan to participate
With joy.
And Freedom.
A Place where
There is nothing but
Truth and love.
And almost a something
That lets go
Of wanting.
And instead loving what is not
It is loving what is.
The ray of the Pacific breeze

Grateful For

Grateful
For the music in my heart.
The kind that coasts through
The rhythm of the day.
That glides with passion
And is still simultaneously
A ribbon of light
That dances within me.
It's a wonderful vision
To be connected.
A ribbon of light
That splashes
And tickles me.
It is the sun.
The ray of the Pacific breeze
Gratitude.

Mana

Is a feeling
A truth I cannot lie.
Mana is in the stillness.
The pause.
Mana is magic.
Mana heals.
Mana is spirit.
Mana is me loving you
Aloha style.
I love mana
And mana loves me.
First I love myself
Then I love you.
Mana gives truth
In the most mystical of ways.
Towards me
It comes in a whisper.

I Can Hear Ocean

Gently rolling
And
A car passes by.
This is Maui
A faint set of birds
Trickle.
Another car lulls by,
I can hear the waves.
The birds faintly sparkle the morning,
It is before dawn.
Another few birds
Appear.
They glisten.
The Pacific is calm here.
I am awed
That all I need to do is listen.
All I hear is beauty.
A twirling set of birds
Enrapture the symphony
As the waves preserve
The integrity.
Carrying the mana
Rhythmically.

Grateful

I am happy

With the life

That is present

With joy.

And relax.

I feel love

In my heart.

Especially in the present moment.

A deep breath

And a sigh.

I am at Peace

With forgiveness.

I can sleep calmly.

Music that calms.

Music that restores

To a new day.

mahalo sun

part two

There Are

Bubbles above the water's surface.
There are ripples in the sand.
When I clench a handful of sand
And release it…
A million little grains
Or perhaps a trillion
Or maybe just a thousand
Glimmer
In the light.
For a Moment.
Under the clean Pacific
I am a magician.
As the Sand
Disappears from me.
Seeping.
The particles glisten.
I swim more and see
Fish.
Real ones.
The kind that I've seen in an aquarium.
The kind that people stare at with awe.

A Diddy For Us

I am seeing me self
In the funniest way
I go upside down
I say hip hoppity horray!
I stand on me feet
They're planted in mud.
They seep in me toes
Yum yummmy yum.
I see a silly you.
I love silly me.
We love silliness
In We.

Swimming

On the mat

Calming to the pace of breath.

Joining together

As one

Cohesive

Tribe.

A slowing

To anew.

Grateful

For the peace.

A time is anew

Thank you .

The Ocean

Rolls
The waves
Subside.
As I Write
Or tap tap on the keyboard.
I crave it.
Calm.
I go to yoga
And my teacher takes me to a place
Inside
Where I am freer to be myself
Unedited.
I am transitioning from the city stimulation
To the calm that Maui brings.
Mother Maui.
The mana
Here
Is real.
I've been typing today and
It's calm.
I ponder

Then interact
And it's different.
Communicating
One human suit
To another.
Face to face
I am grateful again
You giggle
Then I giggle.
And we are all giggling
Together
Under the same sun
It's different
With Zoom.
The room is one
And we are indexed
Yet together.
Virtually we are One.
Thank you for holding space.
It's all virtual
I am awake to this.

Whistle A Whistle

If I whistle
Will you whistle back?
I mean can you whistle?
It's a tune we make
When we are together.
We chitter chatter
Like old friends do.
I liking you
In the most whistling way.
A whistle is a word
That is an onomatopoeia.
It sounds like a special
Sound.
I am present
There's a lot to do.
Keep on whistling
Licking your lips as whistlers do.
And one day I'll be a whistler too.

A Day

That brightens
A glimmer at times.
And then by surprise a golden
Orb.
Fantastic!
It's for all
Fantastic!
It's ours to reap.
And massage in goodness.
It's a light
Massaging the face
With a smile.
From my light to yours
It's ours to share.

Grateful

For your light
When it shares
So openly
So lovingly.
A friend
That is more
Than what
It seems.
A friend
That relishes
What is.
And shares.
It encourages
A wisdom
That reveals
Like a pearl.
Fresh and pristine.
A treasure
To behold.
Something more
When it just is.

It's A Moment

That is right now.
A wonder
When it is
As it is.
And aware of the beauty
That is
Simplicity.

I Love You Like The Rain

It washes and cleanses me each day.
I am fresh.
I am new
To myself.
I am fresh like the rain.
Because of You and you.

Time

I'm a swim to the left
And a swim to the right.
Wiggle
To the rhythm of a time.
It is a gift
To be in the moment.
A gift to be here.
I wiggle
To the beat
Of a place
That is in this moment.

I love to write

It may sound trite
But I love to write
and dance
And sing
And join
Together.
We are whole
Together
We are one
At once.

Moment

A flower.
A simple Moment.
Is calm.
A bee brushing
On a magenta flower.

Home

Where it is
In the Space
Of Time
And Place.
It wanders
Until at last
It is Now.

Afar

Diddle dee
Diddle dee rah.
I see a man who is looking afar…
Into a valley
A glen really.
With dripping dandelions
He's climbing a foot.
A silly shape,
A wonderous way to climb,
Upside down and all around.

A Promise to Promise

To be One
With the source of light.
I see in your eyes
Passion
Truth.
I see oceans
That are clean.
I see time healing
In a World filled with love.
Aloha.

part three

aloha sun

Sunset

Sun set.
Fun set.
Everyone reset!

Chi

I have energy

It's stored.

There's plenty.

Regenerating when I sleep.

Relax.

I am grateful.

I soften.

I am mana.

The spiritual magical mixture of Hawaii.

I breathe a little deeper.

I laugh a little more.

I appreciate.

The details,

The minutea.

I conserve

And preserve.

Every breath of air

Is a gift.

Graditude.

It's A Light

A calm.
Grateful
For humor.
A pleasurable
Way
To be in light.
In a Place
That
Smiles.
It is this Moment
Of Peace
Of Gratitude
That balances
When the light
Is.

She Does

She let me go

To a place of tranquility.

To a place of dignity.

To a place of centering

And light

And truth.

To a place of magic inside

That lightens up

And brightens to the truth of validity

And mighty ness

That is smaller

Than the rest.

That smiles

With a glint

And a bright light.

Beckoning truth

And goodness.

Let's Phone

Let's phone
And chitter chatter for awhile.
The depth of the sea
Is bigger than we.
The length of the tide
Is vast and wide.
I can see a sunrise
Over a cliff.
It is home
To see a shadow
Against the evening bluff.

**And When Your Night Starts
Making Sense**

And the dishes finally get done.
The clothes picked up
Your hair in place.
There's a sigh of relief
To be back in that space.
That is truly your own
A peace that no one can take
Except yourself.
When you remember
Who you truly are
And who you truly matter to
It's worth it all.
And you wouldn't want to trade that
When the dust settles.
And it settles now
Nestled in the moment.

A Lighthouse Keeper

There once was a lighthouse keeper.
A reticent woman who played the harp
As golden as her hair.
The strings stretched flexibly,
Effortlessly as if she did not pluck.
Her fingers danced at times and
Glided at others.
Her husband
A fan.
As his heart skipped and calmed when she
Glides her finger pads on the harp.
Their daughter golden haired
And with a flute.
She summons
At dusk
The ships;
Quelling the sound of seals
Yet alluring ships.
One in particular.

Maui Maui

I can hear the waves
As the drum beats.
I can hear the waves.
A faint gecko beckons
To another perhaps.
I can hear the waves.
I am calm.
At Peace.
I can hear the waves
I am free.

Re Viewing

I am here.
Now what?
I will listen
More.
Gently
To the flow
Of love
That breezes us.
I want to anew myself
Align with Gratitude.
Where a multitude
Is available
Or maybe not.
A treasure.
I am not speaking.
My brain is affirming
And learning.

I am a fixed.

Timing is everything.

I surprise

With warmth.

I am gentle.

I see a light in your eye.

I am grateful.

I soften to the place

Where yawns are.

Sleeping soundly

Peacefully

With birds.

There is a presence

That I long for

A place in this Moment

Namaste.

If I had one wish

I'd wish it for gratitude.
The aptitude
Of gratitude
Multiplies.
Like bubbles
Above the surface.
Transforming
Something so little.
Into a big open shell
Teeming with jewels.
Each one peculiarly brilliant
Each one a gem.

This night

Go gently in this soft night
Fluff up the pillows.
Lie down
Gaze at the constellations
And Mars.
The soft sheets
Buoy you up,
As you drift off
In the bed of your dreams.

thank you

I am grateful to my family, friends, teachers and coaches. The way life goes, each of you fill more than just one role and I thank you. The heart opens easier by being close to the ocean, and each of you keep the Aloha alive. This book is a book because of your support, kindnesses and along the day, you give ways to make the smiles easier and the heart warmer. May you realize how impactful you being yourself brightens and lightens the days. You make poetry flow easier and I thank you. Mahalo

Dad for listening. Mom for encouraging. Laurie for beautiful balance in waves and days. Lucas for being the coolest boy ever. Nicole for being the coolest girl ever. Andrew for honesty. Mimi for believing. Pops for the discipline. Grandma for the music. Aunt Sally for the Focus. Joy for daily sharing. Deni for the mantra and teachings. Michael for supporting, Jing for healing. Kathy for the teachings, Breda your blessings, Michael your recitations. Jeff for keeping it simple, Debbie for dependability. Mojgan for the giggles. Diana for the foresight. Elizabeth for chats, Fionnuala for your loving voicing. Lynne for walks. Frida for keeping it real. Richard for the transformations. Roseanne for the vision. Karen for whimsy. Karen for paddles. Alison for fine tuning. Danielle for the face yoga. Melody for wise gentleness. Mary for compassion. Step for integrity.

Saul for the sage classes. Matthew for grounding.
Kat for reassuring. Jessica for laughing at it all, Amy
for pragmatically poise. Darryl for the realism, Jean
the yogini, Nicki the yogi, June for your sweetness,
Kerri for your spontaneity. Angie for your giving.
Paul for the laughs and Tiki for the stars, Mamma D
for the truth. Brook for the energy. Brooke for the
guidance. Carol for your title untitled. Robert for
your kind posts. Rob for hikes. Selina for the new
ways. Pam for the art, Robert for the kitchen, Sonny
for the laughs. Marci for long time and new times.
Amy for believing, Lizzie for being true. Jen for
patience. Cole for alignment. Patrick for the warmth,
Joseph for the dignity, Nicholene for including,
David for accepting, Anthony for kindness. Cousins
and extended family for the heritage. Shawn for
offering. Roy for the welcoming. To the stewards
for your generosity and Ohana. Jonathan for the
sweetness, Dominick for the guiding. Gentle Thunder
for the videos. Noah for truth. Maui Waveriders:
Tom, Joe, Jen, Monica and the team for opening the
door to morning ocean time. Pro SUP Shop: Cole,
Jen, Steve and the team for opening the door for
morning paddles. Joyce for your creativity, Fredris
for the welcomes. George for getting me there. Tony
for making it happen. Ocean Dancers for the grace.
Ola for the whistles before the ocean, Twoila for
wonderment in the water. And, especially Jane.

www.ingramcontent.com/pod-product-compliance
Lightning Source LLC
LaVergne TN
LVHW021742060526
838200LV00052B/3415